Wainwright

DIARY 2006

FRANCES LINCOLN

Frances Lincoln Limited
4 Torriano Mews
Torriano Avenue
London NW5 2RZ
www.franceslincoln.com

A. Wainwright Diary 2006
Copyright © Frances Lincoln Limited 2005

British Library cataloguing-in-publication data
A catalogue record for this book is available from the British Library

ISBN 0-7112-2488-9

Printed in China
First Frances Lincoln edition 2005

FRONT COVER

THE PATTERDALE VALLEY (*A Fourth Lakeland Sketchbook* 241)

BACK COVER

WATENDLATH (*A Lakeland Sketchbook* 55)

Watendlath is, to many visitors, the epitome of Lakeland. Lying in a hollow of craggy and colourful fells, its old white cottages and farmhouses, tarn, packhorse bridges, waterfalls, ducks and dogs, and the romantic aura bestowed by the novels of Hugh Walpole, cast a lifetime's spell.

TITLE PAGE

SEATOLLER (*A Third Lakeland Sketchbook* 228)

Seatoller, to motorists, is the start of the long climb over Honister Pass; to walkers, it is the place where tired limbs await the Borrowdale bus; to the few people who live there it is (one imagines) the foot of the rainbow.

RIGHT

GREAT END (*A Fourth Lakeland Sketchbook* 291)

The north face of Great End is illuminated by sunlight only at dawn and sunset, and in winter not at all. Its aspect is dark and grim, the gullies appearing as black clefts. The viewpoint is a nameless tarn to the north of Sprinkling Tarn.

CALENDAR 2006

JANUARY
M	T	W	T	F	S	S
						1
2	3	4	5	6	7	8
9	10	11	12	13	14	15
16	17	18	19	20	21	22
23	24	25	26	27	28	29
30	31					

FEBRUARY
M	T	W	T	F	S	S
		1	2	3	4	5
6	7	8	9	10	11	12
13	14	15	16	17	18	19
20	21	22	23	24	25	26
27	28					

MARCH
M	T	W	T	F	S	S
		1	2	3	4	5
6	7	8	9	10	11	12
13	14	15	16	17	18	19
20	21	22	23	24	25	26
27	28	29	30	31		

APRIL
M	T	W	T	F	S	S
					1	2
3	4	5	6	7	8	9
10	11	12	13	14	15	16
17	18	19	20	21	22	23
24	25	26	27	28	29	30

MAY
M	T	W	T	F	S	S
1	2	3	4	5	6	7
8	9	10	11	12	13	14
15	16	17	18	19	20	21
22	23	24	25	26	27	28
29	30	31				

JUNE
M	T	W	T	F	S	S
			1	2	3	4
5	6	7	8	9	10	11
12	13	14	15	16	17	18
19	20	21	22	23	24	25
26	27	28	29	30		

JULY
M	T	W	T	F	S	S
					1	2
3	4	5	6	7	8	9
10	11	12	13	14	15	16
17	18	19	20	21	22	23
24	25	26	27	28	29	30
31						

AUGUST
M	T	W	T	F	S	S
	1	2	3	4	5	6
7	8	9	10	11	12	13
14	15	16	17	18	19	20
21	22	23	24	25	26	27
28	29	30	31			

SEPTEMBER
M	T	W	T	F	S	S
				1	2	3
4	5	6	7	8	9	10
11	12	13	14	15	16	17
18	19	20	21	22	23	24
25	26	27	28	29	30	

OCTOBER
M	T	W	T	F	S	S
						1
2	3	4	5	6	7	8
9	10	11	12	13	14	15
16	17	18	19	20	21	22
23	24	25	26	27	28	29
30	31					

NOVEMBER
M	T	W	T	F	S	S
		1	2	3	4	5
6	7	8	9	10	11	12
13	14	15	16	17	18	19
20	21	22	23	24	25	26
27	28	29	30			

DECEMBER
M	T	W	T	F	S	S
				1	2	3
4	5	6	7	8	9	10
11	12	13	14	15	16	17
18	19	20	21	22	23	24
25	26	27	28	29	30	31

CALENDAR 2007

JANUARY
M	T	W	T	F	S	S
1	2	3	4	5	6	7
8	9	10	11	12	13	14
15	16	17	18	19	20	21
22	23	24	25	26	27	28
29	30	31				

FEBRUARY
M	T	W	T	F	S	S
			1	2	3	4
5	6	7	8	9	10	11
12	13	14	15	16	17	18
19	20	21	22	23	24	25
26	27	28				

MARCH
M	T	W	T	F	S	S
			1	2	3	4
5	6	7	8	9	10	11
12	13	14	15	16	17	18
19	20	21	22	23	24	25
26	27	28	29	30	31	

APRIL
M	T	W	T	F	S	S
						1
2	3	4	5	6	7	8
9	10	11	12	13	14	15
16	17	18	19	20	21	22
23	24	25	26	27	28	29
30						

MAY
M	T	W	T	F	S	S
	1	2	3	4	5	6
7	8	9	10	11	12	13
14	15	16	17	18	19	20
21	22	23	24	25	26	27
28	29	30	31			

JUNE
M	T	W	T	F	S	S
				1	2	3
4	5	6	7	8	9	10
11	12	13	14	15	16	17
18	19	20	21	22	23	24
25	26	27	28	29	30	

JULY
M	T	W	T	F	S	S
						1
2	3	4	5	6	7	8
9	10	11	12	13	14	15
16	17	18	19	20	21	22
23	24	25	26	27	28	29
30	31					

AUGUST
M	T	W	T	F	S	S
		1	2	3	4	5
6	7	8	9	10	11	12
13	14	15	16	17	18	19
20	21	22	23	24	25	26
27	28	29	30	31		

SEPTEMBER
M	T	W	T	F	S	S
					1	2
3	4	5	6	7	8	9
10	11	12	13	14	15	16
17	18	19	20	21	22	23
24	25	26	27	28	29	30

OCTOBER
M	T	W	T	F	S	S
1	2	3	4	5	6	7
8	9	10	11	12	13	14
15	16	17	18	19	20	21
22	23	24	25	26	27	28
29	30	31				

NOVEMBER
M	T	W	T	F	S	S
			1	2	3	4
5	6	7	8	9	10	11
12	13	14	15	16	17	18
19	20	21	22	23	24	25
26	27	28	29	30		

DECEMBER
M	T	W	T	F	S	S
					1	2
3	4	5	6	7	8	9
10	11	12	13	14	15	16
17	18	19	20	21	22	23
24	25	26	27	28	29	30
31						

INTRODUCTION

The exquisite ink drawings in this diary come from the sketchbooks of A. Wainwright, artist, fellwalker and author of the Pictorial Guides to the Lakeland Fells – surely the most original and popular walking guides ever written.

Born in Blackburn in 1907, Alfred Wainwright left school at thirteen to work in the Borough Engineer's office. A holiday to the Lake District at the age of twenty-three kindled a lifelong passion for the fells. Looking back to that visit, he wrote, 'I . . . beheld, from Orrest Head, a scene of great loveliness, a fascinating paradise, Lakeland's mountains and trees and water. That was the first time I had looked upon beauty, or imagined it, even.'

In 1941, Wainwright moved to Kendal, and immediately devoted every spare minute he had to walking the fells which, in due course, turned into research for his first seven Pictorial Guides.

In 1969, *A Lakeland Sketchbook* was published. In typically forthright language, he called it his private rebellion against 'acceptance as art of poverty-stricken and barren inspiration and rank bad execution'. He went on to publish a further twenty-eight volumes of sketches of the landscapes of England, Scotland and Wales. This diary can show only a small selection of his work, but the first five Lakeland Sketchbooks were republished in 2004 and the remaining volumes will be reissued gradually over the coming years. The captions accompanying the sketches in this diary are based on those Wainwright originally wrote. Details of the sketchbooks from which the illustrations are reproduced can be found on the last page.

In 1974, Wainwright became Chairman of Animal Rescue, Cumbria, and, thanks to the book royalties he contributed to the charity, a permanent animal shelter was set up near Kendal. He died in 1991 at the age of eighty-four.

WINDERMERE, AT LOW WOOD

26 Monday
Boxing Day (St Stephen's Day)
Holiday, UK, Republic of Ireland, Canada, USA,
Australia and New Zealand (Christmas Day observed)

27 Tuesday
Holiday, UK, Republic of Ireland, Canada,
Australia and New Zealand (Boxing Day observed)

28 Wednesday

29 Thursday

30 Friday

31 Saturday
New Moon
New Year's Eve

1 Sunday
New Year's Day

JANUARY

2 Monday
Holiday, UK, Republic of Ireland, Canada,
USA, Australia and New Zealand

3 Tuesday
Holiday, Scotland and New Zealand

4 Wednesday

5 Thursday

6 Friday
First Quarter
Epiphany

7 Saturday

8 Sunday

BULLPOT FARM
The lonely, once-deserted farm of Bullpot, high on Casterton Fell, lost its
atmosphere of isolation by the discovery nearby of Lancaster Hole and the Easegill
Caverns – the most complex and extensive cave system in the country, with several
miles of underground passages.

JANUARY

9 Monday

13 Friday

10 Tuesday

14 Saturday
Full Moon

11 Wednesday

15 Sunday

12 Thursday

HARTER FELL, MARDALE

JANUARY

16 Monday
Holiday, USA (Martin Luther King's birthday)

17 Tuesday

18 Wednesday

19 Thursday

20 Friday

21 Saturday

22 Sunday
Last Quarter

BLENCATHRA, FROM CASTLERIGG STONE CIRCLE
The Stone Circle at Castlerigg, often wrongly referred to as the Druids' Circle, is the best-known prehistoric monument in the district, being within easy reach of Keswick and two main roads. Owned by the National Trust and in Government care, the site commands a beautiful and extensive view, Blencathra being especially prominent.

23 Monday

27 Friday

24 Tuesday

28 Saturday

25 Wednesday

29 Sunday
New Moon
Chinese New Year

26 Thursday
Holiday, Australia (Australia Day)

STAC POLLY (STAC POLLAIDH), THE STEEP ROCK OF THE BOG
Visitors to Stac Polly have described its appearance in a variety of imaginative phrases but nobody has bettered Professor Heddle's vivid description of it as 'a porcupine in a state of extreme irascibility'. Its pinnacled and shattered crest is a remarkable example of the effect of weather erosion on sandstone. The word 'unique' is one to use sparingly: here it is very apt. There is no other mountain like Stac Polly.

JANUARY/FEBRUARY

30 Monday

3 Friday

31 Tuesday
Islamic New Year (subject to sighting of the moon)

4 Saturday

1 Wednesday

5 Sunday
First Quarter

2 Thursday

GRANGE IN BORROWDALE
Grange in Borrowdale presents an animated scene on any summer day, the River Derwent here being very accommodating to holiday visitors, providing picnic places, deep pools for the swimmer and shallow inlets for the paddler in the vicinity of the double bridge, while the little cluster of houses, old mingling with new, caters adequately for more material needs. Even more attractive is the winter scene when the encircling fells lie deep in snow.

FEBRUARY

6 Monday
Holiday, New Zealand (Waitangi Day)

10 Friday

7 Tuesday

11 Saturday

8 Wednesday

12 Sunday
Lincoln's birthday

9 Thursday

WASTWATER
You either love Wastwater or are repelled by it. This deepest and most sinister of the lakes can be both frightening and beautiful. It is a black pit in storm, but arrayed in bewitching colours when the dying sun lights its shattered cliffs and screes.

FEBRUARY

13 Monday
Full Moon
Holiday (observed), USA

14 Tuesday
St Valentine's Day

15 Wednesday

16 Thursday

17 Friday

18 Saturday

19 Sunday

HIGH CRAG, FROM HAYSTACKS

FEBRUARY

20 Monday
Holiday, USA (Presidents' Day)

21 Tuesday
Last Quarter

22 Wednesday

23 Thursday

24 Friday

25 Saturday

26 Sunday

LOW FELL, FROM LANTHWAITE HILL
Snow has a remarkable aptitude for greatly increasing the altitude of the
fells, or seeming to. Low Fell near Loweswater hardly gets a second glance
in summer, but in winter, under new snow, it can look Alpine.

FEBRUARY/MARCH

27 Monday

3 Friday

28 Tuesday
New Moon
Shrove Tuesday

4 Saturday

1 Wednesday
Ash Wednesday
St David's Day

5 Sunday

2 Thursday

THE CALDER VALLEY

Road, railway, river and canal jostle for space along the narrow floor of the Calder Valley between Todmorden and Hebden Bridge, and mills and cottages add to the congestion, there being little left to please the eye. Before industry took over, however, the valley was green and threaded only by a clear river and a country lane, and the view of it from the high ground adjoining must have been quite lovely. It is still possible, from vantage points on either side, to imagine the rural scene that has since been destroyed.

MARCH

6 Monday
First Quarter

7 Tuesday

8 Wednesday

9 Thursday

10 Friday

11 Saturday

12 Sunday

NAB COTTAGE, RYDAL
Nab Cottage, overlooking Rydal Water, has literary associations. De Quincey (who later succeeded Wordsworth as tenant of Dove Cottage) and Hartley Coleridge both lived there. The date 1702 appears on a tablet over the door.

MARCH

13 Monday
Commonwealth Day

14 Tuesday
Full Moon

15 Wednesday

16 Thursday

17 Friday
St Patrick's Day
Holiday, Northern Ireland and Republic of Ireland

18 Saturday

19 Sunday

DERWENTWATER
The viewpoint is Brandelhow and the occasion the wonderful winter of
1963–4, when for months Lakeland was gripped by an unbroken frost
under cloudless skies. Derwentwater was a sheet of ice from end to end,
the surface being mantled in snow: a truly glorious scene.

MARCH

20 Monday
Vernal Equinox

21 Tuesday

22 Wednesday
Last Quarter

23 Thursday

24 Friday
Jewish Feast of Weeks (Shavuot)

25 Saturday

26 Sunday
Mothering Sunday, UK
British Summertime begins

THE BUTTERMERE VALLEY

MARCH/APRIL

27 Monday

31 Friday

28 Tuesday

1 Saturday

29 Wednesday
New Moon

2 Sunday

30 Thursday

LANGDALE PIKES, FROM LINGMOOR FELL

3 Monday

7 Friday

4 Tuesday

8 Saturday

5 Wednesday
First Quarter

9 Sunday
Palm Sunday

6 Thursday

THE LOWESWATER VALLEY

APRIL

10 Monday

11 Tuesday

12 Wednesday

13 Thursday

Full Moon

Maundy Thursday

Passover (Pesach), First Day

14 Friday

Good Friday

Holiday, UK, Republic of Ireland,

Canada, USA, Australia and New Zealand

15 Saturday

16 Sunday

Easter Sunday

ST JOHN'S IN THE VALE CHURCH

The tiny church of St John's in the Vale stands amongst trees on the low ridge between Naddle Vale and St John's Vale. Less isolated than of yore, it is no less appealing in its simplicity. At one time it was fashionable for Keswick's visitors to attend Sunday service here, but today's pilgrims carry cameras, not Bibles, to this hallowed place.

APRIL

17 Monday
Easter Monday

Holiday, UK (exc. Scotland), Republic of Ireland,
Canada, Australia and New Zealand

18 Tuesday

19 Wednesday
Passover (Pesach), Seventh Day

20 Thursday
Passover (Pesach), Eighth Day

21 Friday
Last Quarter

Birthday of Queen Elizabeth II

22 Saturday

23 Sunday
St George's Day

BEINN ALLIGIN, SUMMIT NAMED
SGÙRR MHÒR OR SGÙRR NA TUAIGH
The traverse of Beinn Alligin is a popular expedition, and (bypassing its famous
Horns) not beyond the powers of the average walker. The summit is a celebrated
viewpoint. The mountain is perhaps the most beautiful of the Torridon giants
and is perfectly seen from the Shieldaig road, the picture being enhanced by the
wooded promontories and lovely inlets of Loch Torridon.

APRIL

24 Monday

25 Tuesday
Holiday, Australia and New Zealand (Anzac Day)

26 Wednesday

27 Thursday
New Moon

28 Friday

29 Saturday

30 Sunday

HILL TOP, SAWREY
Lakeland has inspired many literary figures of renown, none more endearing than
Beatrix Potter. Hill Top, where the creator of Peter Rabbit wove her simple
fantasies, is now a museum of her effects in the care of the National Trust.

MAY

1 Monday
Early May Bank Holiday, UK and Republic of Ireland

2 Tuesday

3 Wednesday

4 Thursday

5 Friday
First Quarter

6 Saturday

7 Sunday

BEAUMARIS CASTLE
Beaumaris Castle was the last of Edward I's eight Welsh castles. Although a military stronghold, the site chosen for it was not dominant, being little above sea level. In appearance it is more a picture-book or fairy-tale castle than the others, romantic rather than aggressive, skilfully built to a neat symmetrical design and surrounded by a moat – the perfect castle in the opinion of experts. It is open to the public.

MAY

8 Monday

9 Tuesday

10 Wednesday

11 Thursday

12 Friday

13 Saturday
Full Moon

14 Sunday
Mother's Day, Canada, USA, Australia and New Zealand

THE STRID, RIVER WHARFE

The Wharfe, upstream from Bolton Abbey, passes through scenery of unsurpassed beauty, its clear waters meandering placidly under a canopy of foliage. But at one point the river is suddenly confined to a rocky channel so narrow that an active person can stride or jump from one side to the other, a feat NOT to be attempted. This is the Strid, a notoriously dangerous spot where many lives have been lost. The Strid is a place to see, but not too closely.

MAY

15 Monday

19 Friday

16 Tuesday

20 Saturday
Last Quarter

17 Wednesday

21 Sunday

18 Thursday

THE BRECON BEACONS
From whatever direction seen, the Brecon Beacons rise in stately grandeur over a wide area of the National Park, forming a beautiful background to the verdant lowlands around. The loftiest point, Pen-y-fan, reaches 2907 feet and is the highest ground in Wales south of Cader Idris. The Beacons are an extensive wilderness, used at times for military training, and no place for inexperienced walkers. The viewpoint of the drawing is the Promenade at Brecon.

MAY

22 Monday

26 Friday

23 Tuesday

27 Saturday
New Moon

24 Wednesday

28 Sunday

25 Thursday
Ascension Day

THE PATH TO GREENUP
A path that is a joy on a bright summer morning is the rough track leading up the Stonethwaite valley towards the hills. It is untidy and stony, winding its way amongst boulders and tumbledown walls and bracken with the tree-fringed beck nearby, but as a prelude to a day on the tops it is perfect.

29 Monday
Spring Bank Holiday, UK
Holiday, USA (Memorial Day)

30 Tuesday

31 Wednesday

1 Thursday

2 Friday
Jewish Feast of Weeks (Shavuot)

3 Saturday
First Quarter

4 Sunday
Whit Sunday (Pentecost)

SWALEDALE
If there were to be a poll amongst regular visitors to the Dales to see which valley
is adjudged the finest it is probable that weight of opinion would award pride of
place to Swaledale. There may be rivers more charming than the Swale, hills
grander than the dark moors that border it and sweeter woodlands elsewhere, but
no scenes of greater natural harmony, no vistas more lovely, can be found than
those that give such delight to travellers along Swaledale.

JUNE

5 Monday
Holiday, Republic of Ireland
Holiday, New Zealand (The Queen's birthday)

9 Friday

6 Tuesday

10 Saturday
The Queen's official birthday (subject to confirmation)

7 Wednesday

11 Sunday
Full Moon
Trinity Sunday

8 Thursday

THE MOSEDALE HORSESHOE

JUNE

12 Monday
Holiday, Australia (The Queen's birthday)

13 Tuesday

14 Wednesday

15 Thursday
Corpus Christi

16 Friday

17 Saturday

18 Sunday
Last Quarter
Father's Day, UK, Canada and USA

BURNSALL
The delights of Burnsall have often been praised, and this pretty village in the heart
of Wharfedale deservedly has many admirers. A fine bridge, a maypole, tidy streets,
neat cottages, a church with Anglo-Saxon remains, lovely surroundings and, of
course, the river, all contribute to make Burnsall a favoured and a favourite place.

JUNE

19 Monday

23 Friday

20 Tuesday

24 Saturday

21 Wednesday
Summer Solstice

25 Sunday
New Moon

22 Thursday

GRASMOOR
The best place for appraising a mountain is a point opposite at mid-height – rarely can its proportions be fully appreciated when viewed from a valley or from a summit of similar elevation. For this reason, the eastern edge of Mellbreak is a grandstand seat for a study of Grasmoor.

JUNE/JULY

26 Monday

30 Friday

27 Tuesday

1 Saturday
Holiday, Canada (Canada Day)

28 Wednesday

2 Sunday

29 Thursday

CATBELLS AND NEWLANDS

The shy and comely valley of Newlands is for the connoisseur of quiet beauty. It has not the romantic appeal of neighbouring Borrowdale, from which it is separated by the abrupt ridge of Catbells, and it has not the crowds – nor the ice cream and mineral water depots – but here in withdrawn seclusion amongst the hills is a verdant and tranquil loveliness.

JULY

3 Monday
First Quarter

4 Tuesday
Holiday, USA (Independence Day)

5 Wednesday

6 Thursday

7 Friday

8 Saturday

9 Sunday

SGÒR NAM FIANNAIDH, PEAK OF THE FIANNS (FINGAL'S ARMY)

Sgòr nam Fiannaidh, forming the western end of the Aonach Eagach ridge, is the least attractive of the Glen Coe mountains but is notable for, and easily identifiable by, a deep cleft in its southern flank. The viewpoint is the Celtic cross near the village of Glencoe commemorating MacIan, Chief of the MacDonalds, who perished in the massacre of 1692.

10 Monday

14 Friday

11 Tuesday
Full Moon

15 Saturday
St Swithin's Day

12 Wednesday
Holiday, Northern Ireland (Battle of the Boyne)

16 Sunday

13 Thursday

JULY

17 Monday
Last Quarter

18 Tuesday

19 Wednesday

20 Thursday

21 Friday

22 Saturday

23 Sunday

BOARDALE

Cartographers prefer to name this valley Boredale or Bore Dale (while inconsistently conceding that the head of it is Boardale Hause) but writers spell the name Boardale, which seems likelier in the company of so many Grisedales. Nowadays there are no wild pigs, but the valley and its environs on the eastern side of Ullswater are even more enchanting without them, a peaceful backwater of beauty that does not advertise itself, nor needs to.

24 Monday

25 Tuesday
New Moon

26 Wednesday

27 Thursday

28 Friday

29 Saturday

30 Sunday

RYDAL WATER
To be factual, Rydal Water occupies the valley of the Rothay between Loughrigg
Fell and Nab Scar. But it really needs no introduction. Everybody knows it and
everybody goes there. The wardens who collect and remove motorloads of litter
from White Moss Common have no doubt about it.

JULY/AUGUST

31 Monday

1 Tuesday

2 Wednesday
First Quarter

3 Thursday

4 Friday

5 Saturday

6 Sunday

BOWNESS BAY, WINDERMERE

Bowness Bay presents a scene of animation alien to Lakeland, and discerning visitors (in the minority, judging by the Bowness crowds) search for natural beauty elsewhere. Before the tourists came Bowness Bay must have been very lovely. It is still actually rather better than Blackpool.

AUGUST

7 Monday
Summer Bank Holiday, Scotland and Republic of Ireland

8 Tuesday

9 Wednesday
Full Moon

10 Thursday

11 Friday

12 Saturday

13 Sunday

BASSENTHWAITE LAKE
The foot of Bassenthwaite Lake is the haunt of yachtsmen, and their slender craft make a pretty picture as they cruise on its placid waters. The viewpoint of the drawing is the outlet of the lake near Ouse Bridge, where the Derwent resumes its journey from Borrowdale to the Irish Sea.

AUGUST

14 Monday

18 Friday

15 Tuesday

19 Saturday

16 Wednesday
Last Quarter

20 Sunday

17 Thursday

BLENCATHRA, FROM ST JOHN'S VALE

21 Monday

25 Friday

22 Tuesday

26 Saturday

23 Wednesday
New Moon

27 Sunday

24 Thursday

WORMS HEAD

Gower ends abruptly in the towering cliffs of Worms Head and the glorious curve of Rhossill Bay, a fitting climax to a tour of the peninsula. The scenery is dramatically beautiful, and enhanced by a vivid carpet of gorse on the clifftops, along which there is a popular walk from the carpark at the end of the road in the hamlet of Rhossill.

AUGUST/SEPTEMBER

28 Monday
Summer Bank Holiday, UK (exc. Scotland)

29 Tuesday

30 Wednesday

31 Thursday
First Quarter

1 Friday

2 Saturday

3 Sunday
Father's Day, Australia and New Zealand

ULLSWATER AND GRISEDALE

SEPTEMBER

4 Monday
Holiday, Canada (Labour Day) and USA (Labor Day)

8 Friday

5 Tuesday

9 Saturday

6 Wednesday

10 Sunday

7 Thursday
Full Moon

COTTER FORCE
Little known and suffering in patronage from the proximity of the popular Hardrow Force, but well worth the short walk to it from the A684 at the head of Wensleydale, is the lovely stepped waterfall of Cotter Force, displaying its charms perfectly for camera enthusiasts.

SEPTEMBER

11 Monday

15 Friday

12 Tuesday

16 Saturday

13 Wednesday

17 Sunday

14 Thursday
Last Quarter

ROBINSON

Robinson deserves some sympathy for its prosaic name amongst an array of poetic gems like Blencathra and Glaramara and romantic descriptive titles such as Hindscarth and High Stile. It derives from a Richard Robinson, an early landowner, and was first recorded as 'Robinson's Fell'. But what's in a name? This is a grand hill to climb.

SEPTEMBER

18 Monday

19 Tuesday

20 Wednesday

21 Thursday

22 Friday
New Moon

23 Saturday
Autumnal Equinox
Jewish New Year (Rosh Hashanah)

24 Sunday
First Day of Ramadân (subject to sighting of the moon)

CWM PENNANT

Cwm Pennant, reached from the Caernarfon–Porthmadog road, is one of the loveliest of the valleys of Snowdonia, but, because there is no way for cars through the mountains at its head, one of the least frequented. Better than any detailed description, its charms are perfectly expressed in the words of the poet Eifion Wyn: 'Oh God, why didst thou make Cwm Pennant so beautiful and the life of an old shepherd so short?'

25 Monday

29 Friday
Michaelmas Day

26 Tuesday

30 Saturday
First Quarter

27 Wednesday

1 Sunday

28 Thursday

CRUMMOCK WATER

OCTOBER

2 Monday
Jewish Day of Atonement (Yom Kippur)

3 Tuesday

4 Wednesday

5 Thursday

6 Friday

7 Saturday
Full Moon
Jewish Festival of Tabernacles (Succoth), First Day

8 Sunday

OCTOBER

9 Monday
Holiday, Canada (Thanksgiving Day)
Holiday, USA (Columbus Day)

10 Tuesday

11 Wednesday

12 Thursday

13 Friday

14 Saturday
Last Quarter
Jewish Festival of Tabernacles (Succoth), Eighth Day

15 Sunday

MATSON GROUND, WINDERMERE
Indirectly the Windermere district owes much of its prosperous and attractive
appearance to the fruits of commerce. It has long been a retreat, an escape from urban
Lancashire, and many of its fine houses were built by business men in the last century;
or, as in the case of Matson Ground (once a farmhouse), existing buildings have been
adapted and enlarged, and intakes and paddocks transformed into lovely gardens.

OCTOBER

16 Monday

20 Friday

17 Tuesday

21 Saturday

18 Wednesday

22 Sunday
New Moon

19 Thursday

DOVE CRAG

There is unsuspected interest and charm in many of the smaller side-valleys of Lakeland and none rewards a leisurely exploration more than beautiful Dovedale, uninhabited and out of the sight and sound of Patterdale's busy traffic. Hazel woods lead up to a tangle of wild country where massive vegetation-capped boulders lie in chaotic confusion below the overhanging cliff of Dove Crag, inaccessible to all but the most expert of rock climbers.

OCTOBER

23 Monday
Holiday, New Zealand (Labour Day)

27 Friday

24 Tuesday
United Nations Day

28 Saturday

25 Wednesday

29 Sunday
First Quarter
British Summertime ends

26 Thursday

BEN LOYAL (BEN LAOGHAL)
Often referred to as the Queen of Scottish Mountains, Ben Loyal forms a
compelling skyline at the head of the Kyle of Tongue, its succession of granite
peaks towering almost grotesquely above the surrounding moorlands in
magnetically attractive array. From the old road by Lochan Hacoin it presents a
perfect picture, much photographed.

OCTOBER/NOVEMBER

30 Monday
Holiday, Republic of Ireland

31 Tuesday
Hallowe'en

1 Wednesday
All Saints' Day

2 Thursday

3 Friday

4 Saturday

5 Sunday
Full Moon
Guy Fawkes' Day

BOOT

Boot, the 'capital' of Eskdale although no more than a hamlet, has happily preserved its many characteristic features: the old mill by the stream, the packhorse bridge, the one quaint street, the massive walls of pink granite; so that the scene, in its essentials, has changed not at all over the centuries. Gone, however, is a source of former activity with the closing of the iron mine on the fellside and the railway terminus adjoining it, although these abandoned sites still provide lots of interest for visitors.

NOVEMBER

6 Monday

7 Tuesday

8 Wednesday

9 Thursday

10 Friday

11 Saturday
Holiday, Canada (Remembrance Day)
and USA (Veterans' Day)

12 Sunday
Last Quarter
Remembrance Sunday, UK

LANGDALE PIKES, FROM SIDE PIKE

13 Monday

14 Tuesday

15 Wednesday

16 Thursday

17 Friday

18 Saturday

19 Sunday

BLEA TARN
The Blea Tarn that all tourists know (there are others of the same name) occupies a hollow on the neck of high ground linking Great and Little Langdale, and, with its fringe of pines and rhododendrons, makes a perfect foreground to the dramatic backcloth of the Pikes as a century of artists, first with brush and latterly with camera, have told in pictures.

NOVEMBER

20 Monday
New Moon

21 Tuesday

22 Wednesday

23 Thursday
Holiday, USA (Thanksgiving Day)

24 Friday

25 Saturday

26 Sunday

CANISP
Canisp is a bold pyramid of sandstone yet fails to compete in shapeliness with the surrounding mountains of Assynt. It has the misfortune to be a near neighbour of Suilven and is invariably seen in the latter's company; and if Suilven appears in a view nothing else gets much attention. Canisp is the only mountain hereabouts that looks ordinary and capable of ascent by normal fellwalking – which is, perhaps, a merit.

NOVEMBER/DECEMBER

27 Monday

1 Friday

28 Tuesday
First Quarter

2 Saturday

29 Wednesday

3 Sunday
Advent Sunday

30 Thursday
St Andrew's Day

SLIOCH

When Slioch is seen across Loch Maree through the pines of Grudie it is posed perfectly, begging to be photographed. From here its steep buttresses and rocky tower seem impregnable, like a castle in the sky. Legions of passers-by have obliged.

DECEMBER

4 Monday

8 Friday

5 Tuesday
Full Moon

9 Saturday

6 Wednesday

10 Sunday

7 Thursday

TRYFAN, FROM OGWEN

The rocky peak of Tryfan, towering into the sky above the Ogwen valley, is the most challenging of Snowdonia's mountains and its striking outline is the most admired. It also has the roughest terrain, the top in particular being a huge pile of boulders, difficult to negotiate and bounded by precipitous cliffs. Tryfan takes swift revenge on those who do not treat it with respect. But its ascent is an experience that lives long, and happily, in the memory.

DECEMBER

11 Monday

12 Tuesday
Last Quarter

13 Wednesday

14 Thursday

15 Friday

16 Saturday
Jewish Festival of Chanukah, First Day

17 Sunday

BEN NEVIS, FROM TORLUNDY
The most-favoured viewpoint for photographs of Ben Nevis is Corpach, perhaps because of the interesting foreground offered by the quaint buildings on the pier or by the war memorial, but it is not wholly satisfactory because the view includes only the merest suggestion of the great north-eastern cliffs that give the mountain its principle distinction. Moving eastwards from Fort William, these cliffs come splendidly into sight at Torlundy. Although partly obscured by intervening foothills, enough is seen of them to give an appreciation of their splendid architecture.

DECEMBER

18 Monday

19 Tuesday

20 Wednesday
New Moon

21 Thursday

22 Friday
Winter Solstice

23 Saturday

24 Sunday
Christmas Eve

THE ROAD TO WATENDLATH

The most enchanting and romantic of all Lakeland's roads is the narrow byway leaving Borrowdale at Ashness Gate and ending at Watendlath, four miles away in a fold of the hills. If any Lakeland road should be closed for pleasure motoring it is this; but, instead, it has suffered many 'improvements' and the passage of cars has been smoothed and made easier by parking places, the result being summer congestion. Walkers have been diverted to a new footpath to save their skins. The squirrels have fled. There is noise where there was peace and quiet . . .

25 Monday
Christmas Day
Holiday, UK, Republic of Ireland, Canada,
USA, Australia and New Zealand

29 Friday

26 Tuesday
Boxing Day (St Stephen's Day)
Holiday, UK, Republic of Ireland,
Canada, Australia and New Zealand

30 Saturday

27 Wednesday
First Quarter

31 Sunday
New Year's Eve

28 Thursday

LANGDALE PIKES, FROM CHAPEL STILE

ILLUSTRATIONS

The drawings illustrating each week of the diary come from the sketchbooks of A. Wainwright.
The reference number for each sketch follows the title of the sketchbook.

Introduction *A Second Lakeland Sketchbook* 121

Week 52 *A Fifth Lakeland Sketchbook* 375

Week 1 *A Second Dales Sketchbook* 85

Week 2 *A Second Lakeland Sketchbook* 81

Week 3 *A Fifth Lakeland Sketchbook* 327

Week 4 *Scottish Mountain Drawings Vol. 1* 19

Week 5 *A Lakeland Sketchbook* 57

Week 6 *A Third Lakeland Sketchbook* 226

Week 7 *A Third Lakeland Sketchbook* 179

Week 8 *A Third Lakeland Sketchbook* 231

Week 9 *A Second Dales Sketchbook* 147

Week 10 *A Third Lakeland Sketchbook* 219

Week 11 *A Second Lakeland Sketchbook* 101

Week 12 *A Lakeland Sketchbook* 35

Week 13 *A Lakeland Sketchbook* 24

Week 14 *A Fifth Lakeland Sketchbook* 385

Week 15 *A Lakeland Sketchbook* 30

Week 16 *Scottish Mountain Drawings Vol. 1* 58

Week 17 *A Lakeland Sketchbook* 72

Week 18 *A North Wales Sketchbook* 75

Week 19 *A Second Dales Sketchbook* 135

Week 20 *A South Wales Sketchbook* 19

Week 21 *A Fifth Lakeland Sketchbook* 364

Week 22 *A Second Dales Sketchbook* 99

Week 23 *A Fourth Lakeland Sketchbook* 298

Week 24 *A Dales Sketchbook* 57

Week 25 *A Third Lakeland Sketchbook* 200

Week 26 *A Lakeland Sketchbook* 37

Week 27 *Scottish Mountain Drawings Vol. 3* 183

Week 28 *A Fourth Lakeland Sketchbook* 241

Week 29 *A Lakeland Sketchbook* 50

Week 30 *A Third Lakeland Sketchbook* 234

Week 31 *A Fifth Lakeland Sketchbook* 335

Week 32 *A Lakeland Sketchbook* 40

Week 33 *A Lakeland Sketchbook* 54

Week 34 *A South Wales Sketchbook* 45

Week 35 *A Third Lakeland Sketchbook* 163

Week 36 *A Dales Sketchbook* 31

Week 37 *A Fourth Lakeland Sketchbook* 317

Week 38 *A North Wales Sketchbook* 57

Week 39 *A Fifth Lakeland Sketchbook* 344

Week 40 *A Third Lakeland Sketchbook* 215

Week 41 *A Fourth Lakeland Sketchbook* 251

Week 42 *A Lakeland Sketchbook* 73

Week 43 *Scottish Mountain Drawings Vol. 1* 2

Week 44 *A Lakeland Sketchbook* 61

Week 45 *A Fifth Lakeland Sketchbook* 349

Week 46 *A Fourth Lakeland Sketchbook* 307

Week 47 *Scottish Mountain Drawings Vol. 1* 13

Week 48 *Scottish Mountain Drawings Vol. 1* 47

Week 49 *A North Wales Sketchbook* 27

Week 50 *Scottish Mountain Drawings Vol. 3* 152

Week 51 *A Lakeland Sketchbook* 6

Week 52 *A Second Lakeland Sketchbook* 160